Texas Wineries

A Guide
with favorite winery recipes

D1710503

Compiled by Barry Shlachter

© Great Texas Line Press
Post Office Box 11105, Fort Worth, Texas 76110
(800) 73TEXAS

Table of Contents

Winemaking in Texas

Texas wines still startle some people, but that shouldn't be the case. Although made in such unlikely sounding spots as Lubbock and Fort Worth, and once cruelly derided as misguided products of "Chateau Bubba," they are winning recognition and gold medals at the most prestigious competitions. Acclaimed chef Wolfgang Puck has served Lone Star vintages at his Los Angeles restaurant, Spago. So has the White House. *The Wall Street Journal* featured the quality wine produced by Fall Creek Vineyards in tiny Tow, Texas.

After a visit, *Gourmet* magazine wine editor Gerald Asher wrote that it "was immediately clear that Texas winemakers had nothing to explain and even less to apologize for." As far back as 1986, Lubbock's Llano Estacado took a double gold (for a unanimous decision by judges) at the industry-respected San Francisco Fair wine competition.

This is not to say it's been easy for Texas winemakers, who have had to fight not only a baseless public perception but also archaic state laws that crippled marketing efforts, not to mention a panoply of natural enemies – from drought, hail, and freezes to Pierce's disease, nematodes, black rot, cotton rot and spider mite. Then there are such marauding critters as raccoons, rabbits, grasshoppers, porcupines and mockingbirds.

Many pioneers, following the then-prevailing wisdom that European varietal grapes could not thrive in Texas soil, planted hybrids that made poor wine before discovering the experts were wrong.

Now, visitors will find a range of varieties that originated in France, Germany, Italy and Spain. These include Chardonnay, Cabernet Sauvignon, Merlot, Sauvignon Blanc, Viognier, Chenin Blanc, Cabernet Franc, Barbera, Zinfandel, Shiraz, Grenache, Pinot Noir, Mourvedre, Malvasia Bianca, Toscana Rosso, Sangiovese, Gewürztraminer, Riesling, Muscat Canelli, Tempranillo and Port. Whew!

"Growing grapes and making good wine in Texas is

a challenge, something that seems to appeal to the Texas temperament," says wine writer Paul Franson. "Its vintners have demonstrated that they can make good wine, and only time will tell whether it can succeed commercially in an increasingly competitive market."

In 1979, the state's total wine output was a minuscule 12,000 gallons from four wineries.

By 2001, Texas' output totaled 1.45 million gallons from 40 producers, according to Texas Tech University's Texas Wine Marketing Research Institute. In a good year, it ranks fifth in the nation, behind California, New York, Washington and Oregon.

If there's a reason that Texas wines aren't better known, it could be that Texans themselves consume more than 96 percent of the state's output. Texans are proud and, for better or worse, are generally willing to pay a premium for their compatriots' wine.

Texas winemaking is nothing new. The tradition goes back to 1662, when Spanish priests established a vineyard at the Mission Senora de Guadeloupe, which has since been swallowed up by El Paso.

And the French industry owes a debt to Texas researcher Thomas Munson, who helped save many prized vineyards from the *phyloxera* epidemic in the late 19th century by sending over disease-resistant, native-grape root stock.

America's Prohibition snuffed out some 25 Texas wineries, although Del Rio's tiny Val Verde Winery somehow weathered the dry spell. The family-owned winery continues today, just a stone's throw from the Rio Grande, which marks the border with Mexico.

The modern Texas wine industry really began in the 1970s, with numerous small operations opening and closing over the next few decades.

Today, there are six recognized appellations or American viticultural areas in Texas – Davis Mountain, Escondido Valley, Hill Country, Fredericksburg, Bell Mountain and High Plains. A seventh region, Mesilla Valley, is mainly in New Mexico but includes a bit of far West Texas, including El Paso.

Where to go?

If you are visiting Austin

and plan to be in the area, the Texas Hill Country and the separate Fredericksburg/Hill Country offer some of the state's most visitor-friendly towns, many fringed by fields of wildflowers in spring. There are wineries in Fort Davis and Fort Stockton should you be touring Big Bend National Park or nearby Terlingua, home of world-famous chili con carne cook-offs.

The Dallas-Fort Worth Metroplex is a convenient jumping-off point to a number of boutique wineries in Grapevine, which also houses tasting rooms of wineries located elsewhere. From Houston, a few hours' drive puts you in range of wineries in Brenham, College Station, Santa Fe and the Beaumont area.

And should you be in Lubbock, touring one of the area's three wineries – Llano Estacado, Cap*Rock and Pheasant Ridge – could well be the highlight of your visit.

Every attempt has been made to convey the most comprehensive listing of wineries. Let us know if we've overlooked anything that might be of interest to readers.

As a bonus, Texas vintners have shared their favorite dishes, many made with their wines. So, which wine to drink?

Obviously, the quality of the wine is ever-changing due to the characteristics of particular grape crops and how the vintner deals with them. Many established wineries have taken home a passel of prizes, which are noted in the descriptions. And be mindful of award-winning "reserve" wines not sold publicly.

While awards may be a guide to future vintages, they are, as with stocks and mutual funds, no guarantee of future performance.

You could do worse than sampling as many Texas wines as you can, then choosing your favorites.

Santé, y'all!

Barry Shlachter
Fort Worth

The maps were based on information provided by Texas Wine & Grape Growers Association, the Texas Department of Agriculture, and the wineries.

Annual Texas Wine Events

Mid-February	Wine Lovers Trail, Hill Country wineries
Mid-February	Southwest Wine Symposium, Kerrville
Mid-March	Springfest Food & Wine Festival, Old Town Spring
Late March	Dennison Art & Wine Rennaissance, Dennison
Early April	Texas Hill Country Wine & Food Festival, Austin
Mid-April	Texas Wine and Food Festival, San Angelo
Mid-April	Wine & Wildflowers Trail, Hill Country
Mid-April	New Vintage Wine & Art Festival, Grapevine
May	Rockport Festival of Wines, Rockport
Mid-August	Harvest Wine Trail, Hill Country wineries
Mid-September	Grapefest, Grapevine
Early October	Passport Event, Hill Country wineries
December	Holiday Wine Trail, Hill Country

**For this year's dates and details, call (866) 4TXWINE
or check www.gotexanwine.org.**

Central Texas

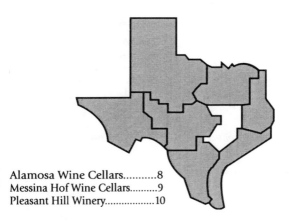

Worth Stopping For:

Colorado Bend State Park, *Bend*, featuring 60-foot Gorman Falls. Tel. (915) 628-3240
George Bush Presidential Library, *College Station*
Cafe Eccell, *College Station*, comfortable off-campus eatery with quality, eclectic fare. (979) 846-7908).

Alamosa Wine Cellars

Located 3 miles west of Bend on Highway 580

677 County Road 430
Bend , Texas 76824
Tel. (915) 628-3313;
(512) 795-87555
E-mail: Jim@alamosawinecellars.com

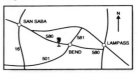

Tasting, tours: By appointment
Varieties: Sangiovese,
Voignier, Tempranillo, Syrah,
Grenache, Mourvedre and
Malvasia Bianca.

Located just west of Bend (near a "V"-shaped bend in the Colorado River) between San Saba and Lamesa, the winery draws its grapes from a 10-acre vineyard. Winemaker Jim Johnson discovered that grapes that produce Spain's prized Rioja are grown in limestone-heavy soil of the sort found on his property, so he planted the same grape, Tempranillo.

And Texas' sultry summers do it no harm. "Unlike the French red grapes, Tempranillo gives rich red colors and good acids even when the weather is really hot," Johnson told the *Austin Chronicle*.

Messina Hof Wine Cellars

From Houston, take U.S. 290 west to Texas 6 North to Bryan. Exit Old Reliance Road in Bryan, turn right. Follow the signs to winery From Austin, Take U.S. 290 east to Hwy. 21 East to Bryan. Exit Texas 6 South. Take Old Reliance Road to the left and follow the signs to winery

4545 Old Reliance Road
Bryan , Texas 77808
Tel. (979) 778-9463, ext. 34
E-mail: wine@messinahof.com
www.messinahof.com

Tastings, tours: Weekdays, 1:00 and 2:30 p.m.; Saturdays 11:00 a.m, 12:30, 2:30 and 4:00 p.m.; Sundays 12:30 and 2:30 p.m.
Varieties: Cabernet Sauvignon, Merlot, Pinot Noir, Gamay, Shiraz, red blends, Muscat Canelli, Gewurtztraminer, Johannisburg Riesling, Chenin Blanc, White Zinfandel, blush blends.

Located on a 100-acre estate, Messina Hof includes a 40-acre vineyard, winery, Vintage House restaurant, guest center, gift shop and the 10-room Villa bed-and-breakfast inn.

The winery's lakeside Guest Center is in the restored Howell House, a local historical landmark and the home of a former U.S. ambassador. His French-style manor was constructed in the early 1900's for the Ursuline Sisters. The rose garden, home to 3,500 white rose bushes, can be rented for weddings and other events.

The villa is adorned with 27 stained glass windows made centuries ago in Spain for a church in Donna, Texas.

Awards: Gold/Star of Texas Grand Award for Merlot '01 , Gold for Johannesberg Riesling '01 and Proprietary Blend '00 (Lone Star Wine Competition). Gold for 2001 Double Barrel Aged Private Reserve Merlot, Silver for 2000 Meritage (2003 Dallas Morning News Wine Competition); Gold for '01 Private Reserve Cabernet Sauvignon, non-vintage Papa Paulo Port Barrel Reserve, '00 Paulo vintage red and '02 Johannisburg Riesling (2003 GrapeFest People's Choice).

Pleasant Hill Winery

**From Brenham: Go south
on Texas 36, right on Salem Road**

1441 Salem Road
Brenham, Texas 77833
Tel. 979-830-VINE (8463)
www.pleasanthillwinery.com
E-mail: info@pleasanthill.com

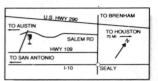

Tastings: Sat. 11 a.m. to 6 p.m, Sun. noon. to 5 p.m.
Tours: 11:30, 12:30, 1:30, 2:30; Sundays 12:30 1:30, 2:30, 3 p.m.
Varieties: Cabernet Sauvignon, Sauvignon Blanc, Chardonnay, Merlot, white and red blends, Ruby and Tawny ports.

The winery, housed in a reconstructed old barn, is situated on scenic rolling hills just south of Brenham. Check its Web site for catered tastings of new releases and other special events, including a wine-grape crush in late July and early August in which visitors can participate. Bring clean feet; expect them to leave purple. Children welcome.

The winery complex includes a gift shop, an extensive collection of corkscrews and wine-making artifacts.

Awards: Silver for non-vintage Collina Bianca (2002 Wine Society of Texas/Media Choice Competition), Silver for non-vintage Tawny Rosso Forte port, Bronze for non-vintage Rosso Forte port (2003 Texas' Best Wine Competition), Gold People's Choice Award for non-vintage Blanc du Bois (2003 GrapeFest), Gold for non-vintage Merlot, silver for '01 Sauvignon Blanc (2003 Lone Star Wine Competition)

Hill Country

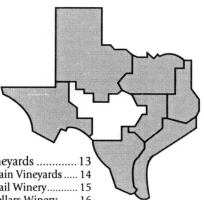

Hill Country

Worth Stopping For:

Rose Hill Manor, *Stonewall*, a replica of an Old South plantationhouse, is an inn with four suites and a reputation for fine dining. Beautiful view of the Pedernales River Valley. Tel. (830) 644-2247. Web site: www. rose-hill,com

Downtown Fredericksburg is home to **The Nimitz Museum** and full of quaint shops, including **Der Kuchen Laden** kitchen utensil store. Nearby Hill Country towns of **Stonewall, Luckenbach, Johnson City** and **Blanco** as well as **LBJ Ranch National Historical Park**. Great Cajun-Greek eats in a Texas honky tonk setting at the **Hilltop Café,** 10 miles west of Fredericksburg. (830) 997-8922

Too much wine? Try **Fredericksburg Brewing Company**, an award-winning brewpub on East Main downtown. Tel (830) 997-1646. B&B upstairs.

Cook's Cottage and Suites B&B, *Fredericksburg*, a Sunday house and cottage form an inn noted for its food. Tel. (210) 493-5101

Alte Welt Gasthof, *Fredericksburg*, a B&B filled with European antiques. Tel. (888) 991-6749.

Fredericksburg Herb Farm serves soups and sandwiches for weekday lunches, full weekend menus. Tel. (830) 997-8615.

Becker Vineyards

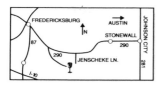

**Located 10 miles east of
Fredericksburg, off U.S. 290
on Jenschke Lane**
U.S. 290 on Jenschke Lane.
Stonewall, Texas 78671
Tel. (830) 644-2681
Mail: P.O. Box 393
www.beckervinyards.com
e-mail: beckervyds@fbg.net

Tasting, tours: Mon.-Thurs. 10 a.m.-5 p.m., Fri.-Sat. 10 a.m.-6 p.m.; Sun. 12 p.m.-6 p.m. Closed on major holidays
Varieties: Cabernet Sauvignon, Chardonnay, Fumé Blanc, Gewürtztraminer, Mouvedre, Merlot, Muscat Canelli Amabile, Syrah, Riesling, Vintage Port, Vioginer.

Surrounded by Fredericksburg's famous peach orchards, grazing quarter horses and fields of Provencal lavender stands the 10,000-square-foot winery, built in to the fashion of a 19th century German stone barn. Adjacent is a log cabin, circa 1880, which serves as the Homestead Bed and Breakfast inn. A bottle of Becker wine comes with a room.

The 36-acre vineyards were established in 1992 with its first commercial harvest three years later. The vines are drip-irrigated with water drawn from limestone formations 300 feet beneath the surface.

The tasting room, decorated with antiques and works by local artisans, includes a large stone fireplace and the original bar from San Antonio's 19th-century Green Trees Saloon. The estate boasts the largest underground wine cellar in Texas, where each vintage matures in French and American oak barrels.

Richard and Bunny Becker expanded their operations with the purchase of the Bluebonnet Hill Vineyard in Ballinger in 1997. The enterprising couple planted 3 acres of lavender behind their main vineyard in 1998 for commercial sale. Visitors are welcome to use the picnic facilities and browse in the gift shop.

Awards: Gold medals for its Merlot '98 and '99, Cabernet Sauvignon Reserve '98 (San Antonio Express-News); Chardonnay Estate '99; Chardonnay '01, Claret '98, Riesling '99, Fume Blanc '00 and Vintage Port '97, Voignier '00, Chenin Blanc '01; Cabernet Sauvignon Reserve/Best of Show-Gold (Wine Society of Texas, Media Choice); Gold for Cabernet Sauvignon Reserve '99 and '01, Merlot '00 (Lone Star Wine Competition); Gold for 2001 Fume Blanc, Silver for "under $16 Chardonnay," Gold for Reserve Cabernet Sauvignon "over $20", Gold for "over $16 red blend" 2000 Claret, Silver for dry Riesling (Texas' Best Wine Competition)

Bell Mountain Vineyards

Located 14 miles north of Fredericksburg on Hwy 16N
1463 Bell Mountain Road
Mail: PO Box 756
Fredericksburg, TX 78624
Tel. (830) 685-3297
www.bellmountainwine.com

Tasting, tours and sales: Saturdays, 10 a.m. to 5 p.m., first Saturday of February through last Saturday of December. Also by appointment 24 hours in advance. Fredericksburg tasting room: Oberhof Winery & Wine Cellar, Located 1.5 miles south of Fredericksburg's Main Street, at 1406 South U.S. 87. (830) 997-0124. Hours: Mon-Sat 10 a.m.-6 p.m., Sun noon-6 p.m.
Varieties: Fume Blanc, Cabernet Sauvignon, Chardonnay, Gewürztraminer; Red Kristkindl, Spiced, Peach, Pinot Noir, Johannisberg Riesling.

Located on the slopes of Bell Mountain, in an area designated in 1986 as Texas' first wine-growing area by the federal government. The vineyard is planted on 56 acres of sandy-loam soils, replete with rich minerals, and blessed with a moderate climate due to its elevation.

Aside from varietal wines under the Bell Mountain label, Bob and Evelyn Oberhelman also produce a spiced red wine, a berry-strawberry-grape wine, a grape-peach wine and mead, fermented from Texas wildflower honey under the Oberhof Wine label. Their Vina Rita line includes a wine margarita and wine piña colada beverages.

The operation includes a wine and gourmet food shop.

Awards: Silver for '01 Late Harvest Riesling (2002 People's choice/Grapefest); Bronze for 2001 Late Harvest Riesling (2002 Texas' Best Wine Competition); Gold for '02 Late Harvest Riesling (2003 GrapeFest People's Choice)

Chisholm Trail Winery at Spring Creek

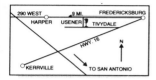

Located 2.5 miles south on Usener Road from U.S.290 West, 9 miles west of Fredericksburg

2367 Usener Rd.
Fredericksburg, Texas 78624
Tel. (830) 990-2675;
(877) 990-CORK
www.chisholmtrailwinery.com
e-mail: chisholm@ctesc.net

Tasting, tours: Thurs.-Mon. noon to 6 p.m., and by appointment
Varieties:: Cabernet Sauvignon, Cabernet Franc, Merlot, Chenin Blanc, Sangiovese, a white Merlot, dessert Cabernet Sauvignon, red blend, Rosé, Muscat Canelli

Located nine miles west of Fredericksburg near pastures dotted with Texas longhorn cattle and wildflowers, the cattle drive-themed winery began production in 1999 and opened to the public in 2001. It uses grapes primarily produced at its 24-acre Spring Creek Vineyards.

The new, rock-walled winery with covered patio will have a restaurant, delicatessen and wedding chapel. Picnickers can sit down along the creek and enjoy the grounds, which include apple and plum trees. See Web site for monthly winery events, ranging from Old West hayrides to formal dinners. Available for private occasions.

The Williams, Paula and Harry, maintain a civil law practice on the site. Between cases, "Trail Boss" Harry minds the vineyards, and Paula and Sabina Comstock does the winemaking.

But they're not alone at the 23-acre vineyard, situated on an 80-acre ranch. There are 33 cattle, five horses, three pot-bellied pigs, eight llamas, hundreds of cats, five dogs and one peach-faced conure.

Awards: Silver for '99 Cabernet Sauvignon ('01 Grapefest); bronze for '00 Merlot ('02 San Antonio); Silver for '01 Sangiovese ('02 Houston Area Restaurants); bronze for '01 Chenin Blanc ('02 Lone Star).

Comfort Cellars Winery

Located in downtown Comfort
723 Front Street
P.O. Box 324
Comfort, Texas 78013-0324
Tel/Fax (830) 995-3274

Tasting, tours and sales: Tasting room is open Mon.-Sat. 12 p.m. to 6 p.m. Sun. noon to 5 p.m. Winery tours by appointment.
Varieties: Merlot, Pinot Noir, Chenin Blanc, Muscat Canelli and a blush, which is a blend of Merlot and Muscat Canelli.

Located across from the post office in downtown Comfort, a quaint, antiques shop-clogged Hill Country town northwest of San Antonio.

The winery is a block from Comfort's historic district. The first vines were planted in 1996, yielding a harvest three years later. Wine can be purchased at the winery.

Driftwood Vineyards

Located 6 miles south of Dripping Springs on Ranch Road 12
21550 Ranch Road 12
Driftwood, Texas 78619
Tel. (512) 858-4508
Web site: www.driftwoodvineyards.com
E-mail: wine@driftwoodvineyards.com

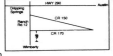

Tasting, tours: Friday and Saturday, 11 a.m. to 6 p.m., Sunday 12:30 to 6 p.m. Other days by appointment. Varieties: Cabernet Sauvignon, Chardonnay, Chenin Blanc, Muscat Blanc, Syrah, Viognier, Sangiovese and Pinot Noir..

Located just west of Austin between Wimberly and Dripping Springs, the relatively new winery is built on a hilltop that affords beautiful views.

It began operations in 2002 on an 880-acre ranch while the adjoining vineyard was planted in 1998 by Kathy and Gary Elliott. Tours, tastings and sales offered.

The winery has its own B&B and holds a September event, The Gathering.

Award: Silver for '02 Viognier ('03 Texas' Best Wine Competition).

Dry Comal Creek Vineyards

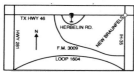

Located 6.6 miles west of New Braunfels off Texas 46 on Herbelin Road
1741 Herbelin Road
New Braunfels, Texas 78132
Tel. (830) 885-4076
Tel. (830) 885-4121
Web site: www.drycomalcreek.com
E-mail: howzr@swbell.net

Tasting, tours: Tastings and sales Wed. through Sun. 12 to 5 p.m. Wheelchair accessible
Varieties produced: Sauvignon Blanc, Chardonnay, Cabernet Sauvignon, French Colombard, Cabernet Franc, Merlot, Rosé,. red and white blends.

Located in a small, protected valley in the Texas Hill Country, Dry Comal grows it grapes on rich alluvial soil laced with limestone, flint and shale chips.

Winemaker Franklin Houser and his wife take pride in their "handmade" approach to cultivation, grape handling, winemaking, cellaring and bottling since selling their first bottle in 1999. To them, achieving ``Texas-style'' wine means producing vintages that retain, fruit, flower, mouth feel and smoothness.

Awards: Silver medals for '01 Cabernet Sauvignon, '01 Merlot, '00 Sauvignon Blanc (Lone Star Wine Competition) Merlot '00, (2002 Texas Open International Wine Competition).

Fall Creek Vineyards

Located 2.2 miles north of Tow's post office
1820 County Road 222
Tow, Texas 78672
Office Tel. (512) 267-6310
Winery Tel. (915) 379-5361
www.fcv.com

Tastings, tours: Monday-Friday, 11 a.m. to 4 p.m.; Saturday noon to 5 p.m.; Sunday noon to 4 p.m. Contact winery for holiday hours and numerous events.
Varieties: Chardonnay, Cabernet Sauvignon, Merlot, Chenin Blanc, Sauvingon Blanc, Johannesburg Riesling, Muscat Canelli, White Zinfandel, Carnelian, and such blends as Granite Reserve (Cabernet-Merlot), Granite Blush, Sweet Jo (Riesling-Muscat), Vintner's Cuvee (Chardonnay-Chenin Blanc), Meritus (Merlot-Cabernet-Malbec).

Located in the scenic Texas Hill Country on the northeastern shore of Lake Buchanan, the winery and vineyards began in 1975 as a pioneer in the state's reborn industry on the Auler family's Fall Creek Ranch, which has a microclimate comparable to those of some of the finest French wine-growing areas.

Hundreds of awards later, Fall Creek has built a reputation for combining the latest growing and winemaking techniques to produce some of the state's most loved wines. Many years, demand outstrips supply for the products of the vineyard's 65 trellised acres, the Aulers say.

The Los Angeles Times

said: "Today their Fall Creek winery is one of the state's best and most consistent." *Wine Spectator* declared Fall Creek's '97 Sauvignon Blanc a "best buy."

Picnickers are welcome to the ranch-based winery and vineyards. The winery sells mustard, jelly, salad dressing and salsa made with its wines.

Awards: Gold medals for '00 Granite Reserve Cabernet and '99 Merlot ('02 Wine Society of Texas Media Choice); Gold for '99 Reserve Chardonnay, Gold/ Best of Class for '94 Sauvignon Blanc (Lone Star Wine Competition) Gold for '98 Merlot (Wine Society of Texas, Springfest Wine Competition); Gold/ Best of Show for '94

Flat Creek Estate

Located off Ranch-to-Market 1431 6 miles west of Lago Vista. Turn south on Singleton Bend Road, go 2.5 miles to Singleton Bend East. Turn left, go 3/4 of a mile to bottom of hill and vineyard is on the left. Turn up the gravel road 1/8 mile to the gated entrance.

24912 Singleton Bend East, Unit 1
Marble Falls , Texas 78654
Tel. (512) 267-6310
www.flatcreekestate.com
e-mail: info@flatcreek.com

Tastings, tours: Tues. through Fri., 12 p.m. to 5 p.m., Saturday and Sunday, 10 a.m. to 4 p.m. Group tours by appointment.
Varieties: Semillon/Sauvignon Blanc blend, Merlot, Sangiovese, Pinot Grigio, Muscat Canelli, Cabernet Sauvignon, Muscato Blanco.

The owners must be nice folk. Sixty friends and relatives turned out in April 2000 to plant 6,000 vines on six acres in six hours flat. Rick and Madelyn Naber, Nebraskan transplants, did their best to re-create a corner of Italy's famed Tuscany in the Texas Hill Country.

And why not? Italian vintages seem to thrive in Lone Star soil hereabouts. Flat Creek grows Sangiovese, Primitivo, Tinta Madeira, Pinot Grigio and Muscat Canelli. In addition, Muscat Blanco and Shiraz grapes also are cultivated.

And there's more than just wine. Reserve a place for a Tuscan-style lunch or dinner, then a hayride or a self-guided tour through the estate's vineyard trail. B&B lodging is planned.

Nestled in a scenic hillside area not far from Travis Peak in the Texas Hill Country, the winery opened in April 2002, and began selling wines produced with grapes from other Texas growers under the Travis Peak Select label.

Award: Silver for '02 Travis Peak Muscato D'Arancia (2003 GrapeFest People's Choice).

Fredericksburg Winery

Located in the Fredericksburg historic downtown area

247 W. Main Street
Fredericksburg, Texas 78624
Tel. (830) 990-8747
Fax (830) 990-8566
www.fgbwinery.com
E-mail: wine@fbgwinery.com

Tasting, tours: Monday-Thursday, 10 a.m. - 6 p.m.; Friday-Saturday, 10 a.m. to 8 p.m.; Sunday 12 p.m. to 6 p.m..
Varieties: Sherry, Port, Hamburg, Scheurebe, Ehrenfelser, Muscat and Orange.

The German-flavored Hill Country community, named for Prince Frederick of Prussia, has a wealth of shops and wineries, including this boutique operation located smack dab on the main drag, Main Street. Interested in a late harvest dessert wine? This is the place.

The Switzer family concentrates on sherries and dessert wines. Making them in small case lots, the little winery-that-could has earned some national med attention.

Some of its wines are traced to far West Texas. The family has secured the leas on the Pecos experimental vineyard established by the University of Texas and renamed it the Old Spanis Trail Research Vineyard. Its winemaker offers an introductory wine course.

Award: Gold-Star of Texas Grand Award for Orange Muscat '00 (Lone Star Wine Competition

20

Grape Creek Vineyard

Located on U.S. 290 at South Grape Creek, 4 miles west of Stonewall, or 9 miles East of Fredericksburg
P.O. Box 102
Stonewall, Texas 78671
Tel. 830-644-2710
Fax 830-644-2746
www.grapecreek.com

Tasting, tours: Mon.-Sat.10 a.m. to 5 p.m.; Sun.12 p.m. to 5 p.m. Tour fee charged.
Varieties: Chenin Blanc, Fume Blanc, Riesling, white blend, Sangiovese, Merlot, Cabernet Sauvignon, Muscat Canelli and red blend.

Located 4 miles west of Stonewall, selected for its beneficial microclimate, the winery's 17 acres of vinifera vines are planted on rolling hills also boast some of the area's famous peach trees, an herb garden and a blackberry patch.

Grape production began in 1985, and after a nearby winery did well with their harvest, Ned and Nell Simes decided to produce their own wine, building this facility in 1989. A year later, they created the first Texas underground wine cellar and an on-grounds B&B (complimentary bottle of wine but no pets, children or smoking) and gift shop for its fans.

The couple, joined by their son's wife and children, have had to weather freezes and rootstock disease, necessitating a major replanting program. The upheavals led to their production of a medium-bodied dry wine, which became their flagship Cabernet Trois.

Grape Creek participates in many of the Hill Country Wine Trail events.

Awards: Gold for '00 Merlot (2003 Texas' Best Wine Competition); gold for '02 sweet Muscat Canelli, sil;ver for '01 Cabernet Blanc and '02 sweet Riesling and bronze for '01, Sangiovese (2003 San Antonio Express-News Competition); silver for '98 Cabernet Trois (2000 Texas Food & Wine Classic; Grapefest People's Choice Award); Bronze for '00 Chenin Blanc (2003 Texas Open Wine & Food Festival); bronze for '01 Cuvee Blanc and '01 dry Riesling (2003 Texas Best Wine.)

McReynolds Winery

From Austin: Texas 71 West to Hamilton Pool Rd, 24 miles to Cypress Mill, right on FM 962, 1 mile to Shovel Mountain Road. From San Antonio: North on U.S.281 to Round Mountain Road, 6 miles East on FM 962 to Shovel Mountain Road.

706 Shovel Mountain Road
Cypress Mills, Texas 78654
Tel. (830) 825-3544

www.mcreynoldswines.com
e-mail: info@mcreynolds.com

Tastings on Saturdays and Sundays, noon to 5 p.m. and by appointment
Varieties: Chenin Blanc, Cabernet Sauvignon, Merlot, Ruby Cabernet, Sauvignon Blanc and Rose of Chenin.

Come by for a small, informal tasting with winemakers Maureen and Mac McReynolds, who learned the craft in California while keeping their day jobs – in scientific research at Stanford University. When weather is good, enjoy the wine with your picnic lunch under the winery's oaks.

After winning a gold medal in 1997 for their Texas Shiraz, the McReynolds decided to make the leap and go commercial with grapes purchased from around Texas and later from those now grown on four of their own acres.

The winery, located 40 miles west of Austin, is home to a Chihuahua named the Brown Bomber.

Awards: Bronze for '00 Cabernet Sauvignon ('02 Wine Society of Texas/ Media Choice Competition)

Pillar Bluff Vineyards

Go 3.5 miles southwest of Lampasas on FM 1478, then left on Burnet County Road 111 for 1/4 mile

300 Burnet County Road 111
Lampasas, Texas 76550
Tel. (512) 556-4078
www.pillarbluff.com

Tastings on Saturdays, noon to 5 p.m. and by appointment
Varieties: Merlot, White Merlot, Chardonnay, Chenin Blanc and Cabernet Sauvignon.

One of Texas' newest wineries, Pillar Bluff is located just west of Lampasas – a little more than an hour northwest of Austin in the Hill Country.

Sample its vintages in the tasting room or outside in the shade of majestic live oaks.

Awards: Bronze medal for '00 Chardonnay (Lone Star Wine Competition), Silver for '01 Merlot (Wines of the South/Knoxville, Tenn.)

Sister Creek Vineyards

Located 12 miles north of Boerne on FM 1376
1142 Sisterdale Road
(Farm Road 1376)
Sisterdale, Texas 78006
Tel/Fax (830) 324-6704
www.sistercreekvineyards.com
e-mail: sistercreek@hstc.net

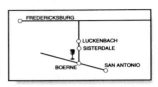

Tastings, tours: Sun.-Thur. noon to 5 p.m., Fri. and Sat. 11 a.m. to 5 p.m.
Varieties: Chardonnay, Pinot Noir , Merlot, Muscat Canelli, red blend.

Located between the cypress-lined East and West Sister Creeks in the Texas Hill Country town of Sisterdale (Pop. 25), and betwixt Boerne and the fabled metropolis of Luckenbach, the winery is housed in a restored 1885 cotton gin.

Now, instead of processing everyone's favorite fiber, Sister Creek crafts such famed French varietals as Chardonnay, Pinot Noir, Cabernet Sauvignon blend, and Merlot in the Bordeaux and Burgundy winemaking techniques. It also produces Italian-style Muscat Canelli.

Sisterdale began as a community of "free-thinking" German immigrants known as the Latin Colonies. They studied in Latin and disavowed organized religion.

In 1988, a century and a half later, a winery was established not far from one believed to have been built by the early European settlers.

Awards: Gold/Star of Texas Grand Award for '01 Muscat Canelli, gold for '00 Chardonnay (Lone Star Wine Competition)

Spicewood Vineyards

From Austin: Take Texas Hwy 71, heading west past Exxon station for 1/2 mile to Burnet County Road 408 and turn left (south), away from the lake. Go about 7/10 mile, turn right on the first road, which is County Road 409. Go 1-1/2 miles through the vineyard, take the left fork. Winery parking is on the right.

Directions from San Antonio. Take U.S. 281 north to Texas 71, then go east toward Austin. County Road 408 is about 8 miles from the intersection of U.S. 281 and Texas 71. Turn right (south) on County Road 408. Go about 7/10 miles, turn right on County Road 409. Go 1-1/2 miles through the vineyard, and take the left fork. Winery parking is on the right.

1419 Burnet County Road 409
P.O. Box 248
Spicewood, Texas 78669

Tel. (830) 693-5328
www.spicewoodvineyards.com

Tastings, tours: Wed.-Sun., noon to 5 p.m.
Varieties: Chardonnay, Semillon, Sauvignon Blanc, Merlot, Cabernet Sauvignon, Cabernet Franc, Zinfandel and blends.

Located west of Austin near Marble Falls, the original winery was handcrafted to resemble a 19th-century Hill Country home with a comfortable front porch and opened for business in 1995.

Outgrowing the structure, a new winery was built four years later with 5,000 square feet on two stories. The upper level provides space for a tasting and special events room, which can be used for weddings and other special occasions. The bottom story houses a 400-barrel cellar.

A covered pavilion and a water fountain grace the grounds. A shaded area is perfect for sipping wine and picnicking while taking in picture-postcard views of the vineyard and the surrounding Hill Country.

Check the winery's Web site for its gourmet dinners and other special events throughout the year. It also displays art and offers organic produce from a local farmer

Awards: Gold/Best of Show for '98 Sauvignon Blanc ('00 Texas Wine Society Media Choice); Silver for '98 Sauvignon Blanc (Los Angeles County Fair) Silver for '96 Merlot ('98 Lone Star Competition);

Texas Hills Vineyard

Located one mile east of Johnson City on RR 2766, the road to Pedernales State Park

Mail: P. O. Box 1480
Johnson City, Texas 78636
Tel. (830) 868-2321
Fax (830) 868-7027
www.texashillsvineyard.com

Tastings: Mon.-Sat., 10 a.m. to 5 p.m.; Sun. noon to 5 p.m. Tours on request
Varieties: Merlot, Syrah, Cabernet Sauvignon, Cabernet Franc, Chardonnay, Pinot Grigio, Sangiovese, Moscato and blends.

A mile east of Johnson City near Pedernales Falls State Park, Gary and Kathy Gilstrap planted 35 acres of vineyards. The couple, both former pharmacists, and son Dale Rassett, built a winery with two-foot-thick walls of rammed earth; the tasting room walls are a foot-and-a-half thick.

Specializing in Italian varieties, it is the first Texas winery to produce an estate Pinot Grigio. The Italian influence comes from the pleasure the proprietors take in its prize-winning Tuscan-style wines, which they produce along with well-known French varieties.

All of them, the Gilstraps promise, are "wines to share with friends."

Check the winery's Web site, or call to find out about their gourmet Italian dinner events on the grounds. The couple encourages picnicking on the patio.

Awards: Gold medal for '00 Cabernet Sauvignc and '01 Moscato (2002 San Antonio Express-News Wine Competition) Silver for '98 Merlot, '00 Rosato and '00 Moscato (2002 Wine Society of Texas/Media Choice Competition); Gold for '01 Moscato, Silver for '01 Tre Paesano "red blend over $16," Bronze for 2001 Rosato di Sangiovese dry rose (2003 Texas' Best Wine Competition)

Wimberley Valley Wines

2825 Lone Man Mountain Road
Driftwood, Texas 78619
Wimberley Valley Wines, Inc.
www.wimberleyvalleywinery.com
Tel. (512) 855-2093

Tours: No public tours at present
Tasting room: located at 206 Main Street, Spring, Texas, north of Houston, East of IH 45, exit
FM 2920. **Hours:** Tue.-Sat. 10 a.m. to 5 p.m., Sun. noon to 5 p.m.
Varieties: Blended white and red wines, including sangria and spiced varieties.

Located between Wimberley and Driftwood among century old live oaks, it has expanded twice since 1982, using grapes grown in Lubbock and Fort Stockton.

After fermenting, aging and bottling, the wines are shipped to the winery's tasting room in Old Town Spring north of Houston, where its vintages and those from other Texas and California vintners are sold, along with gourmet treats.

Woodrose Winery

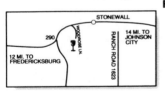

From Fredericksburg: go 12 miles east on U.S. 290, turn right on **Woodrose Lane**
662 Woodrose Lane
Stonewall, Texas 78671
Tel. (512) 663 7404
Tel. (830) 644-2111
www.woodrosewinery.com
e-mail: wood @fbg.net
Tastings, tours: Call for current hours
Varieties: Cabernet Sauvignon and a Cabernet Rosé.

The winery made its first release September 2002, and its new lodge with tasting room is available for special occasions.

With 60 acres of scenic meadows, the grounds are perfect for Texas Hill Country sunrises and sunsets, says contractor-turned-winemaker Brian Wilgus.

West Texas

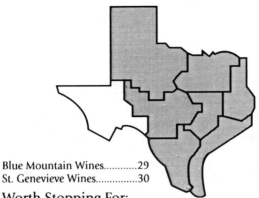

Worth Stopping For:

Davis Mountains State Park, Tel. (432) 426-3337;
Chihuahuan Desert Research Institute, Tel. (915) 364-2499
Fort Davis National Historic Site, Tel (432) 426-3224
McDonald Observatory, Tel (877) 984-7827

The town of **Marfa**, famous for its mysterious night sky lights, as backdrop for the James Dean/Elizabeth Taylor film **Giant**, has galleries and a noted museum of modern sculpture.

Limpia Hotel, *Fort Davis*, built in 1912 for summer visitors to the cool Davis Mountains with pleasant gardens, restaurant-bar and gift shops. Tel (800) 662-5517.

Indian Lodge, Davis Mountains State Park, *Fort Davis*, Full-service hotel built in 1930s by the Civilian Conservation Corps. Tel (432) 426-3254.

Prude Ranch, *Fort Davis*, a historic dude ranch with rooms and bunkhouses and RV campgrounds; indoor pool, tennis courts, gift shop, trail rides, hiking, birding, cafeteria-style restaurant. Tel. (800) 458-6232. E-mail: prude@ overland.net

Veranda Country Inn, *Fort Davis*, once the Lempert Hotel on the Overland Trail stagecoach route, the circa 1883 B&B offers serene gardens and antique-filled rooms. Tel. 888) 383-2847.

Blue Mountain Wines

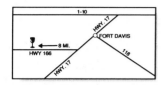

Located eight miles west of Fort Davis on Texas 166

Mail: HCR 74 Box 7
Fort Davis , TX 79734
Tel. (915) 426-3763

Tasting, tours: Tours by appointment; tastings on Tues.-Sat. afternoons
Varieties of wine produced: Cabernet Sauvignon, Merlot, Chenin Blanc and Sauvignon Blanc.

Located in the Davis Mountains on a steep 20 acres at an elevation of 5,300 feet, the Blue Mountain winery is situated in one of the best microclimes for wine grape growing in Texas. The vineyard was planted in 1977.

Nearby are dude ranches, power-generating windmills, a frontier fort once manned by legendary Buffalo soldiers, the McDonald Observatory and the historic Limpia Hotel, where the wine is served in a comfortable dining room.

Awards: Silver medals for Cabernet Sauvignon '00 and Red Table Wine 01' (Lone Star Wine Competition); Bronze for '00 Cabernet Sauvignon (2002 GrapeFest People's Choice); Silver for non-vintage Blue Mountain Red (2003 GrapeFest People's Choice).

Ste. Genevieve Wines

Located on McKenzie Road Crossover

Mail: P. O. Box 697
Fort Stockton, Texas 79735
Tel (432) 395-2417

**Tastings, tours: By appointment
on Wednesday and Saturday
mornings, arranged through the
Fort Stockton Chamber of
Commerce. (800) 336-2166.**
Varieties: Chardonnary, Merlot, Cabernet Sauvingon, Pinot Noir, blush blend.

Texas' largest winery almost since its inception in 1987, Ste. Genevieve is situated near a 867-acre vineyard owned by the University of Texas Land Office. The growing region has been designated Escondido Valley, one of the state's six American viticultural areas, which were established along the lines of France's venerable appellation zones.

Ste. Genevieve, originally launched by two French and two Texas partners, produces vintages ranging from value-priced but prize-winning, 1.5-liter blended table wines to its more up-scale Escondido Valley line of varietals.

Like many Texas wineries, it has had a rocky history. At one point, the University of Texas Land Office managed the operation when the original partners fell out and the bank foreclosed. Under new owners, it considers itself among the state's most successful wineries, selling 500,000 cases a year.

Awards: Gold for non-vintage Chardonnay and silver for non-vintage Cabernet Sauvignon (2002 Lone Star Wine Competition) Bronze for non-vintage Chardonnay (2003 Dallas Morning News Wine Competition).

East Texas

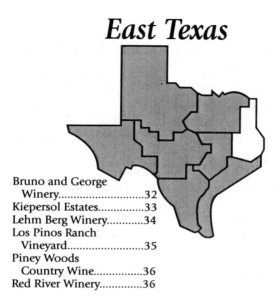

Worth Stopping For:

Big Thicket National Preserve (An arc stretching north and west from ***Beaumont***.) Hiking, camping, biking, horseback riding, canoeing, bird-watching, fishing. UNESCO Biosphere Reserve since 1981 and named a Globally Important Bird Area in 2001. Visitor center in ***Kountze.*** Tel. (409) 246-2337

Ethridge Farm B&B, ***Kountze,*** a log-cabin inn in a restful setting. Tel. (409) 898-2710 or (409) 246-3978; Fax: (409) 898-2710. www.ethridgefarm.com

Pelt Farm B&B, ***Kountze,*** an 1840 log dog-trot cabin with antique roses, butterflies, large oaks, Choctaw horses and yellow blackmouth cur dogs. Tel. (409) 287-3300. www.peltfarm.com

Spindletop-Glady City Boomtown, ***Beaumont,*** re-creation of an early oil-strike boomtown. Tel. (409) 835-0823.

Bruno & George Winery

From Beaumont: Take Texas 105 to Sour Lake. At red light, turn left on Texas 326, left on Old Beaumont Road before the elementary school. Turn right on Nevada Street and drive to end, then right on Messina Road and follow it to the winery.
From Houston: Take US 90 E to Nome, Texas. Turn left on Texas 326 and continue north about 6.5 miles to Sour Lake, then right on Old Beaumont Road. Follow road until Nevada Street, then right and travel to end; turn right on Messina Road and follow it to the winery.

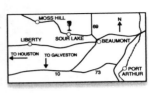

400 Messina Road
Sour Lake , Texas 77659

Tel. (409) 898-2829,
(409) 963-8235
www.brunoandgeorge.com

Tastings: By appointment.
Varieties: Raisin, peach, blueberry, pear, strawberry.

This small establishment, 18 miles west of Beaumont, is at the forefront of resurrecting the old art of raisin winemaking, illegal in Texas until a 1999 law removed dried fruit from a list of banned ingredients for commercial wine.

Raisin wine goes back nearly 3,000 years and has been made without interruption for centuries in Italy. This winery's technique was borrowed from an old Sicilian family recipe brought over by one of the founder's grandfathers.

Award: Bronze for Tawny Port Raisin Wine (2003 Texas' Best Wine Competition)

Kiepersol Estates Vineyards

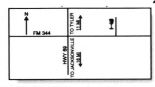

**Located 11 miles south of Tyler
on FM 344E.**
3933 FM 344 E.
Tyler, Texas 75703
Tel. (903) 894-8995
Fax (903) 894-4140
www.kiepersol.com

ting, tours: Mon.- Fri. 9 a.m.-1 p.m., 2 p.m.- 5 p.m.
urdays 11 a.m. - 6 p.m.
rs by horse and buggy by appointment; $10/person or $60 minimum; by van, $5 per person.
ieties: Cabernet Sauvignon, Shiraz/Syrah, Barbera and Sangiovese.

In a gated community south of Tyler, 14 acres of vineyards were planted in 1998 and 1999, with the first harvest in 2000. The wines are aged in French and American oak barrels.

The winery boasts not only an upscale restaurant and 5-room bed and breakfast inn, but also a chapel for use by overnight guests for private worship. The quaint brick edifice can be reserved for small weddings, exchanges of vows and christenings.

The restaurant features prime and choice beef, fresh seafood and a wine list with 150 vintages, including the estate's own.

Awards: Bronze for 2000 Merlot (2001 Lone Star Wine Competition); Bronze for 2001 Syrah (2002 Wine Society of Texas).

Lehm Berg Winery

Located between Austin and Houston off U.S. 290, or between Waco and Victoria on U.S. 77

1266 County Road 208
Giddings , Texas 78942
Tel. (979) 542-2726;
Fax (979) 542-0082
www.lehmbergwinery.com
E-mail: LehmBergWinery@bluebon.net

Tastings: Mon-Fri 4-6 p.m.; Sat. 11 am-6 p.m.; Sun. noon- 5 p.m. Tours: By appointment
Varieties: Merlot, Lenoir, Blanc du Bois, Riesling, Primitivo (Zinfandel), Muscadine, blush, strawberry, raisin and native Mustang.

Located between Houston and Austin, the winery uses modern techniques to replicate the Droemer family's homemade wines of the 1900s.

The winery, established in 2002, is found in a 1927 house made of red bricks fired in a down-draft kiln right on the property, reflecting the family's brick-making heritage. The estate's old smokehouse has been transformed into an aging cellar where wines mature in oak barrels.

The wines are made from grapes and fruit grown locally and elsewhere in Texas, resulting in a unique down-home character and taste. The Droemers offer tastings, and a gift shop on the premises sells locally made crafts. An original round smokehouse is an added feature.

Check the winery's web site about periodical wine tasting classes, wine and food pairings and other events

Los Pinos Ranch Vineyard

Located 5 miles south of Pittsburg, 2 miles west of U.S. 271

658 County Road 1334
Pittsburg, Texas 75686
Tel. 903-855-1769
www.lospinosranchvineyards.com

Tastings, tours: Friday through Sunday, noon to 10 p.m.
Varieties: Blanc du Bois, Cynthiana, Muscat
Canelli, Cabernet Sauvignon.

Located five miles south of Pittsburg amid the lush greenery of East Texas' Camp County, the winery and vineyard were established by a couple transplanted from California. They found immediate acceptance; their 2002 Blanc du Bois sold out in five weeks.

Nearly every month brings an event featuring food and music to accompany the Sneed family's wine. Contact the winery or its web site for information.

Blanc Du Bois
TEXAS   2002   TABLE WINE

Piney Woods Country Wines

From Houston: head east on Interstate 10, take exit 875, head west to Tejas Parkway to Willow Drive
3408 Willow Drive
Orange, Texas 77632
Tel. (409) 883-5408

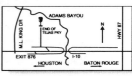

Tastings: Mon.-Sat., 9 a.m.-5 p.m. Tours: Groups only and by appointment. There is a charge for guided tours.
Varieties: Muscadine, Blueberry, Strawberry, Plum, Pear, Peach and Orange.

Nestled in the woods near Adams Bayou, Piney Woods has specialized in "country wines" since selling its first batch in 1987. Vintner Alfred Flies produces seven varieties of Muscadine wine aside from his fruit wines.

Awards: Silver for non-vintage Plum Wine and Noble (Wine Society of Texas/Media Choice Competition); Silver medal for Light Ruby Port (2002 Lone Star Wine Competition).

Red River Winery

Head east on Main Street to Gentry Street in Old Town Spring

421 Gentry #204
Spring, Texas 77373
Tel. (281) 288-9463
www.redriverwinery.com
e-mail: redriverwinery@msn.com

Tastings: Tue.-Sat., 10 a.m. - 3 p.m.; Sun. noon - 3p.m.
Varieties: white and red blends.

Located in Old Town Spring 20 miles north of Houston, this quaint storefront winery has been blending, cellaring and bottling its own wine since 1995.

It sells all sorts of wine accessories and will custom label your favorite vintages.

North Texas

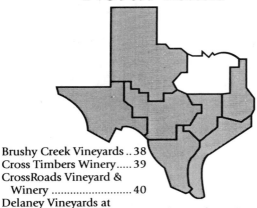

Worth Stopping For:

Cow Camp Steakhouse (between Alvord and Decatur on Texas 287) an upscale steak place. Tel. (940) 627-7741

Heritage Inn B&B Cluster, *Denton,* three Victorian houses restored as an inn. Tel. (840) 565-6414.

Second Monday Trade Days, *Bowie,* actually held Friday-Sunday before the second Sunday; five acres of flea market with 452 vendors.

Historic Wise County Courthouse, *Decatur,* a little gem built of pink limestone in1895; two good lunch places on the square. Mattie's and Courthouse Café are both popular with residents.

Bison Hollow, *Aubrey,* a log cabin B&B on 16 wooded acres. Full country/southwestern breakfast. Horse stalls. Tel. (940) 365-9460

Brushy Creek Vineyards

From Fort Worth: Go north on Interstate 35, then north on Texas 287, exit County Road 2798, a mile north of Alvord

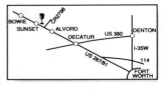

572 County Road 2798
Alvord, Texas 76295
Tel. (940) 427-4747; 427-4718
e-mail: brushyck@wf.net

Tasting, tours: Tasting room 10 a.m. to 6 p.m.., or by appointment. Tours by appointment
Varieties produced: Merlot, Cabernet Sauvignon, sweet red blend, Ruby Port.

Located about 50 miles northwest of Fort Worth between Decatur and Bowie in Texas' historic Cross Timbers area, Brushy Creek Vineyards was founded in 2002 by Les Constable, a retired nuclear engineer-turned-vintner who had won awards as a amateur vintner, inspiring him to go commercial.

Wines from numerous other Texas wineries are for sale in gift and tasting shop. The Southwestern adobe-looking winery is built in the side of the hill.

Cross Timbers Winery

Located in Grapevine's downtown area

805 Main St.
Grapevine, Texas 76051
Tel. (817) 488-6789
Fax (817) 488-7981
e-mail: crosstimberswinery@directlink.com
www.crosstimberswinery.com

Tasting, tours: Mon.-Sat. 12 p.m. to 5 p.m. Sun. 12:30 to 5 p.m.
Varieties: Chardonnay, Merlot, Cabernet Sauvignon and blush.

Located in an 1874 shotgun, Prairie-style Brock House in Grapevine, the winery opened in 2001 and sells its own vintages as well as imported wine and wines from other Grapevine producers. Deli meals are available on request.

The owner, self-taught winemaker Don Bigby, says he bought the building without telling his wife, Penny. She knows now.

A two-story "party barn" is available for weddings and other special occasion with a 200-person capacity along with a gazebo and demonstration vineyard.

Awards: Gold for '00 Blush (2002 People's choice/Grapefest); Gold for non-vintage Blush (2003 GrapeFest People's Choice).

CrossRoads Vineyards & Winery

From Fort Worth: Take Interstate 35W north to Loop 288, east to Texas 380, go east 10 miles to County Road 424, turn left and go north to Fish Trap Road, turn right; second farm on left.

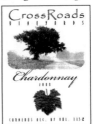

8400 Fish Trap Road
Crossroads , Texas 76227
Tel (940) 440-9522
Fax (940) 365-9451
Web site: www.crossroadsvineyards.com
e-mail: laura@crossroadsvineyards.com

Tasting, tours and sales: Thur.-Sun. 1 p.m. to sunset. Tours and tastings at other times by appointment.
Varieties: Fumé Blanc, Dry Muscat Canelli, Chardonnay, Muscat Canelli, blush, red blend, Merlot, Cabernet Sauvignon, sweet red, Tawny Port.

Located 30 miles north of Dallas, the winery and 3-acre vineyard share 50 acres with ducks, geese, goats, llamas and a stocked fishing pond. The boutique, 4,000-square-foot winery and cellar is dedicated, owners Laura and Fernando Sanchez say, to "making fine Texas wine."

Find out for yourself at their pool-side gazebo tasting bar, where their numerous wine varieties are served. Gifts and gourmet condiments offered for sale.

Relatively new,

CrossRoads opened for business in 2001. Picnicking encouraged.

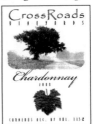

Award: Bronze medal for Reserve Chardonnay '00 (2002 Lone Star Wine Competition); Bronze for '00 Merlot ('02 Southwest Wine Competition, Ruidoso, NM).

Delaney Vineyards at Grapevine

From Fort Worth: Take the Glade exit on Texas 121 heading north toward Grapevine
2000 Champagne Blvd.
Grapevine, Texas 76051
Tel. (817)481-5668
www.delaneyvineyards.com

Tasting, tours: Saturdays, 12 p.m. to 5 p.m. Weekdays by appointment. Tours free, tasting $7 per person
Varieties: Cabernet Sauvignon, Chardonnay, Muscat Canelli, Merlot, Sauvignon Blanc, Claret, Rosé, white table wine, and dry sparking wine made in the champenoise manner.

Just off Texas 121 near DFW International Airport stands one of the state's most eye-catching wineries with slate roof, cathedral ceiling and skilled stone masonry, giving a very European accent to a corner of North Texas.

It is built to resemble an 18th century french winery with a 5,200 square-foot, grand barrel room where the wine is aged in oak.

Delaney's finest can be enjoyed at the far end where an Italian granite tasting bar stands. Around the corner is a cute gift shop with wine-related items. Private labeling of wine per request.

Winery grounds are available for weddings and special events.

Awards: Bronze for non-vintage Sparkling Wine and Texas Rose (Lone Star Wine Competition); Silver for non-vintage Texas Claret and Texas Rose (2002 People's Choice/Grapefest); Gold for non-vintage Texas Claret (2003 GrapeFest People's Choice).

41

Hidden Springs Winery

From Denton: Go east on
Texas 360, north on Texas 377
256 North Texas 377
Pilot Point , Texas 76258
Tel. (940) 686-2782
www.hiddenspringswinery.com

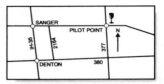

Tasting, tours: October - Dec. 24., Tues.- Sat. noon - 5 p.m., 2 p.m. to 5 p.m., rest of the year Tues.-Sat. Noon to 5 p.m. or by appointment; Daily tours available at 3:30 p.m. Please make reservations for parties of 10 or more.
Varieties: Merlot, Cabernet Sauvignon, Chardonnay and blends.

Housed in a Victorian-style, antiques-filled house (a former catfish restaurant), the 33,000-square-foot winery is the dream of winemaker Lela Banks. She was inspired by a trip to Europe, where she found people producing homemade wine. The 1994 graduate of France's Clos du Vougeot course, and her husband, a retired airline pilot, launched the winery in 1996 with profits from their Whitesboro vineyard and aquatic nursery.

The establishment boasts a tasting room with mammoth, century-old oak bar. A study in Victorian warmth, the winery's gift shop offers crafts, gourmet foods and its own wines. A special events room is available.

Awards: Gold for '94 Cabernet Sauvignon ('97 Lone Star Wine Competition), Gold/Best of Class for '95 Cabernet Sauvignon (Lone Star), Silver for '97 Cabernet Sauvignon (Lone Star) Gold for '95 Chardonnay ('97 Grapefest People's Choice), Gold for '94 (Grapefest People's choice), Gold for Crystal red table wine ('97 Lone Star); Silver for Crystal Red Table Wine ('98 Lone Star), Silver for Blush ('97 & '99 International Eastern Wine Competition), Silver/Best of Class for Blush ('98 Lone Star),Silver for Vintner's Red ('99 Lone Star), Silver for Vintner's White and for '97 Muscat Canelli ('00 Wine Society of Texas).

Homestead Winery

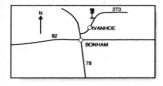

Located 8 miles north of Bonham

County Road 2041
Mail: P. O. Box 35
Ivanhoe, Texas 75447
Tel (903) 583-4281

Tours: By appointment
Denison tasting room at 220 W. Main Street
Tel. (903) 464-0030
Hours: Wed.-Sat. 11 a.m.-5 p.m

Grapevine Tasting Room at 211 E. Worth
Tel. (817)251-9463
Hours: Wed.-Sat. 11 a.m.-5:30 p.m., Sun. Noon-5:30 p.m.
Varieties: Chardonnay, Cabernet Sauvignon, Sherry, Port, Blush, Muscat Canelli, Bois d'Arc.

The family-owned winery planted its vineyard in 1983 on a former wheat farm and began producing wine in 1989. Its owners' forebears have farmed in the region for more than a century.

Aside from wine, the Grapevine tasting room on historic Main Street also displays and sells works of local artists. The Denison tasting room is similarly located in the historic downtown.

Awards: Gold/Star of Texas Grand Award/White Wine for non-vintage Rosé of Ivanhoe (2001 Lone Star Wine Competition), Gold for non-vintage sweet Rosé of Ivanhoe, Bronze for non-vintage Dessert Rosé ('02 People's Choice/Grapefest); Silver medal for Homestead Red ('02 Lone Star Wine Competition); Silver for non-vintage Rose of Ivanhoe and non-vintage Desert Rose (2003 GrapeFest People's Choice).

La Bodega

At D/FW International Airport, 26 miles northeast of Fort Worth; 27 miles northwest of Dallas Terminal A, opposite Gate 15 Dallas-Fort Worth International Airport

Mail: P. O. Box 613136
D/FW Airport, Texas 75261
Tel. (972) 574-4351

Varieties: Merlot, Chardonnay, Cabrenet Sauvignon, blush.

Perhaps the only winery in an airport, La Bodega might be the perfect place to unwind after a full-body-and-shoe search between flights. The micro-winery on 430 square feet is the brainchild of Gina Puente-Brancato, an entrepreneur with other concessions at the airport. She was elected president of the Texas Wine and Grape Growers Association in 2003.

The award-winning wines are made in collaboration with Messina Hof Winery of College Station and are served in a relaxing environment along with more than 30 other Texas wines. A gift shop sells wine-related merchandise. The winery's labels depict Father Garcia de San Francisco y Zuniga, father of Texas wine-making, who produced the first Lone Star vintage at Mission Senora de Guadeloupe near El Paso in 1659.

Awards: Silver medals for Chardonnay '00 and Merlot '00 (Lone Star Wine Competition); Gold for '01 Reserve Merlot Silver for '01 Reserve Cabernet Sauvignon (2002 People's Choice/ Grapefest); Silver for 2000 Red Zinfandel, Silver for 2001 Chardonnay "under $16;" Bronze for 2001 Cabernet Sauvignon (2003 Texas' Best Wine Competition); Silver for '01 Private Reserve Cabernet Sauvignon and '01 Private Reserve Merlot (2003 GrapeFest People's Choice).

La Buena Vida Vineyards

From Fort Worth, go northwest on Texas 199 past Springtown center, left on Old Springtown Road, go 3.4 miles to Mill Road, turn left and go 3/4 miles, right on Vineyard Lane

La Buena Vida Vineyards #1
650 Vineyard Lane
Springtown, Texas 76082
Tel. (817) 220-4366

From Grapevine center, north on Main Street, left on College Street

La Buena Vida Vineyards #2   Tel. (817) 220-4366
416 East College   www.labuenavida.com
Grapevine , Texas 76051   e:mail: lbv@labuenavida.com

Tastings, tours in Grapevine: Mon-Sat, 10 a.m.-5 p.m., Sun noon to 5 p.m.
Tours in Springtown: By appointment.
Varieties: Cabernet Sauvignobn, Merlot, Chardonnay, Sauvignon Blanc, White Merlot, White Zinfandel, Muscat Canelli, Port, Champagne-style sparkling wine, and honey-based mead and Texmas Blush.

Dr. Bobby Smith established one of the first modern-era Texas wineries in 1972 when he established an organic operation in Springtown, later expanding to Grapevine, which is attracting an ever-wider pool of visitors seeking Lone Star wines. He christened his venture La Buena Vida (The Good Life), and it has brought much joy to regional drinkers and garnered a few prizes along the way.

Smith is Texas' longest-running continuous producer of methode champenoise sparkling wine, made in the manner in which French Champagne is produced. Wine grapes are grown in Springtown, then crushed for its brands – Springtown, Grapevine, La Buena Vida, Smith Estate and Walnut Creek Cellars.

The winery's Grapevine tasting room is in a

limestone former church in the historic district. It is furnished with an antique bar, salvaged from a 1920s-era Dallas hotel, fountains, herb gardens and a winery museum. The grounds are available for special events.

Each winter, Smith and his staff present "Wine 101," a wine appreciation course, and "A Day at the Winery," a hands-on rundown of wine-making with barrel tastings.

WALNUT CREEK CELLARS
RESERVE
1985
TEXAS PORT

PRODUCED AND BOTTLED BY LA BUENA VIDA VINEYARDS
650 VINEYARD LANE, SPRINGTOWN, TEXAS 76082
CONTENTS 375 ML.   ALC. 18% BY VOL.

Awards: Gold medal for Vintage Old/Chambourcin reserve port '85 (2002 Lone Star Wine Competition); Gold/Star of Texas Award for non-vintage Springtown Muscat Dulce (2001 Lone Star), silver or '98 Springtown Cabernet Sauvignon ('00 Indy International).

Light Catcher Winery

From Fort Worth: Texas 199 (Jacksboro Hwy), turn left on Confederate Park Road, go 1.8 miles.

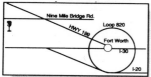

6925 Confederate Park Rd.
Fort Worth Texas 76135
Tel. (817) 237-2626
Office: (817) 237-0137
www.lightcatcher.com
e-mail: lightcatch@aol.com

Tasting, tours: Wed.-Sun., noon to 5 p.m. Free tour; charge for tasting four wines with keepsake glass.
Varieties: Merlot, Cabernet Sauvignon, Chardonnay, Merlot Rosé.

This quality boutique "microwinery" holds many events, including new vintage release parties. Contact them when you plan to be in the vicinity. The winery includes an art gallery, assembles gift baskets with wine and gourmet treats, and sells quality stemware.

Caris Turpen, a transplanted Californian and Emmy-award-winning cinematographer, always loved winemaking and decided to make her ambition a reality when she moved to the Fort Worth area with her native Texan husband, Terry. Samplers of her wine will be convinced she made the right decision.

"Winemaking is art and science, stirred by mystery," insists Caris. Check the winery's Web site for numerous events, incorporating art, m food and wine.

Having quickly outgrowned their original winery, the Turpens relocated on 4 acres of live oak groves and gardens, where in 2003 they built a tile-roofed, rock-walled Tuscan-style winery. Look for a meditation labyrinth, ponds, outdoor sculptures and art on display in the tasting room. The building and grounds are available for special events.

Awards: Silver for '02 Nouveau Merlot (semi-dry Rose) (2003 Texas' Best Wine Competition); Bronze for '01 Texas Roads Chardonnay (2003 Dallas Morning News Wine Competition); Bronze for the '02 Merlot Rose (2003 Lone Star International).

Lone Oak Vineyards

Take the FM3002 Exit on Interstate-35 north of Denton

4781 East Lone Oak Road
Valley View , Texas 76272
Tel. (940) 637-2612 or 2222
e-mail: loneoak@texoma.net

**Tastings: Thurs-Sat, 2 p.m. to
7 p.m., or by appointment.
Tours: By appointment**
Varieties: Merlot, Cabernet Sauvignon and red blends.

A small Bordeaux-style vineyard in the rolling hills of North Texas between Denton and Gainesville, Lone Oak ages its wine in French oak barrels, then hand-bottles the vintage in classic St. Emilion style.

Lone Oak offers on-site catering; check with the winery about events.

Awards: Silver for '99 Merlot (Wine Society of Texas/Media Choice Competition); Silver medal for Merlot '00 (Lone Star Wine Competition); Bronze for 2001 Merlot more than $16 (2003 Texas' Best Wine Competition)

Wales Manor Vineyard & Winery

4488 County Road 408
McKinney, Texas 75071
Tel. (972) 542-0417
e-mail: wales@airmail.net

Tastings, tours: Closed to the public.
Varieties: Cabernet Sauvignon, Merlot, Chardonnay, Muscat Canelli and Sauvignon Blanc.

In a rural corner of Collin County, just north of Dallas, a winery with a 10,000-case capacity has been built near a three-acre vineyard growing Cabernet Sauvignon grapes. It opened for business during its August 2003 crush.

48

Wichita Falls Vineyards & Winery

From Fort Worth: Go north on Interstate 35W to U.S. 287 North, pass Wichita Falls and take Peterson Road Exit, head south and at fork onto Peterson Road South

3399 Peterson Road South
Iowa Park, Texas 76367
Tel. 940-855-2093
Fax 940-851-5022
e-mail: a1969l@aol.com

Tastings and tours: Sat. 10 a.m. to 6 p.m., and other times by appointment
Varieties: Cabernet Sauvignon, Merlot, Sangiovese, Zinfandel, White Zinfandel, late-harvest Cabernet Port and blends.

In 2003, one of the state's newest wineries was opened several miles west of Wichita Falls by Alton and Lana Gates, a regional utility manager and kindergarten teacher, respectively. It is located amid 300 native pecan trees near the junction of the Wichita River bottom and Buffalo Creek, not far from Horsehoe Lake.

The winery is housed in a functional metal building with a second-story balcony.

Wines are classically aged in oak casks, both American and French, while Hungarian oak barrels are used for its Port. The winery has a gift shop and a room available for special events.

High Plains

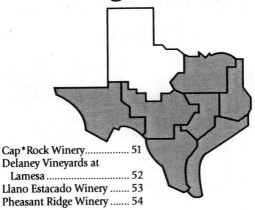

Worth Stopping For:

National Ranching Heritage Center, *Lubbock*, located on the Texas Tech campus. Tel (806) 742-0497.
Buddy Holly Statue and Walk of Fame, *Lubbock*, at the entrance to the Civic Center. (806) 767-2241.
Prairie Dog Town, *Lubbock*, in Mackenzie State Park, within the city limits. Tel. (806) 767-2687.
Broadway Manor, *Lubbock*, a B&B housed in a 1926 mansion in the historic Overlook section. Tel. (877) 504-8223. www.broadwaymanor.net

Cap＊Rock Winery

Located east of U.S. 87 on Woodrow Road about 5 miles south of Lubbock
408 East Woodrow Road
Mail: Route 6, Box 713K
Lubbock, Texas 79423
Tel. (806) 863-2704
www.caprockwinery.com

Tasting, tours: Visitor center Mon-Sat from 10 a.m.-5 p.m., Sunday from 12:00 p.m. until 5:00 p.m. (In addition, the winery has a tasting room and gift shop in Grapevine, 409 South Main Street, northeast of Fort Worth. Tue-Sat from 11 a.m.- 4:30 p.m.

Varieties: Cabernet Sauvignon, Cabernet Royale (rose of Cabernet Sauvignon), Chardonnay, Merlot, and blends including Toscano Rosso (Sangiovese, Barbera and Cabernet Sauvignon, Topaz Royale (Chenin Blanc, Riesling and Muscat Canelli), Orange Muscat, a fortified dessert wine, and Blanc de Noir sparkling (champenoise method).

The state-of-the-art winery was built in 1988, its distinctive architecture inspired by Spanish missions. Featuring 40-foot ceilings and manicured grounds, it is 5 miles south of Lubbock in Texas' Great High Plains, which has turned out to be fine wine country as well as paradise for countless prairie dogs. The wine is sold in Texas, New York, California, France and Switzerland.

For years, Cap＊Rock's has garnered awards and "best buy" recommendations for vintages crafted by winemaker Kim McPherson, a Lubbock native and son of Dr. Clinton "Doc" McPherson, an early Texas wine pioneer who helped establish nearby Llano Estacado Winery. Surviving the ups and downs of the state's wine industry, Cap＊Rock has consistently beaten the odds and has been rewarded with a slew of well-earned awards.

The attractive winery can be booked for weddings, meetings and other special occasions. Aside from a tasting room in Lubbock and another in Grapevine, northeast of Fort Worth, the winery has a gift shop. On-site sales are permitted.

Awards: More than 400 awards,including, Gold for '00 Cabernet Sauvignon "under $20," for 2001 Chardonnay "under $16", Silver for dry white blend 2001 Palo Duro Canyon White (Texas' Best Wine Competition); Silver for '01 Blush Royale (2003 GrapeFest People's Choice).

Delaney Vineyards
at Lamesa

**Located on Texas 137,
one mile north of Lamesa**

Lamesa, Texas 79331
Tel. (806) 872-3177

Tasting, tours: By appointment
Varieties: Cabernet Sauvignon, Chardonnay, Muscat Canelli, Merlot, Sauvignon Blanc, Claret, Rose, white table wine, and dry sparking wine made in the champenoise manner.

On what was once a cotton farm, 87 acres of grapevines were planted and now produce 12 varieties of quality wine grapes. Unfortunately, this neck of the woods is "dry," so the wine cannot be sold at the facility, but tastings are permitted.

Awards: Bronze for Texas High Plains sweet rosé non-vintage (2003 Dallas Morning News Wine Competition); Gold for non-vintage Texas Claret (2003 GrapeFest People's Choice).

Llano Estacado Winery

Located 3.2 miles east of U.S. 87
South on Farm Road 1585

Mail: P.O. Box 3487
Lubbock, Texas 79452
Tel. (806) 745-2258
e-mail: info @llanowine.com
www. llano.com

Tours and tastings: Mon.-Sat. 10 a.m.-5 p.m.; Sun. noon-5 p.m.
Tasting room in Grapevine at 1000 South Main, Suite 252
Varieties: Chenin Blanc, Johannisburg Riesling, Chardonnay, Passionalle, Cabernet
Sauvignon, Port, Merlot and various blends.

Located in Buddy Holly
country, traditionally better
known for prairie dogs,
cotton growing and Texas
Tech, the winery launched
by two Tech professors in
1976 has proved that very
drinkable wine can be
produced in the Lone Star
State. Its premium wine can
be found in more than 20
states and in seven countries
in Asia and Europe. Llano
vintages have been served
at the White House under
the two most recent Texas
presidents.

The vineyards are planted
at an elevation of 3,200 feet
on the Texas High Plains,
where native Americans
and Spanish explorers once
roamed. The grapes mature
during warm days and cool
nights like those of the finest
French growing regions.

Llano shook up
the California wine
establishment when its
1984 Chardonnay snared a
Double Gold (for unanimous
decision) at the 1986 San
Francisco Fair competition,
the nation's prestige event.
That and other prizes have
built a loyal following for its
premium vintages.

Awards include Gold for Chardonnay '01,
silver for Johannesburg White Riesling
'01, Signature Red 00', Port (2002 Lone
Star Wine Competition); Gold/Best of
Class & Grand Star of Texas Award for
'00 Chardonnay Double gold for '84
Chardonnay (1986 San Francisco Fair
wine competition); Gold for '00 Cellar
Select Chardonnay and '87 Viviano
(Wine Society of Texas/Media Choice
Competition); Gold for '01 Cellar Select
Chardonnay, Gold for '02 Signature White
(blended white), Gold for '01Passionelle
Shiraz/Rhone blend (2003 Texas' Best
Wine Competition).

Pheasant Ridge Winery

From Lubbock: go north on Interstate 27 north and take exit #14, travel east 2 miles to winery sign, turn south and go 1 mile to find winery on the left

Mail: Route 3, Box 191
Lubbock, Texas 79401
Tel (806) 746-6033; 34;
Fax: (806) 746-6750
www.pheasantridgewinery.com

Tasting, tours: Fri- Saturday, noon to 7 p.m., Sun.1 p.m. to 5 p.m. Other times by appointment.
Varieties: Merlot, Chardonnay, Cabernet Franc, Pinot Noir, Chenin Blanc, Cabernet Sauvignon, blended white and red.

Located northeast of Lubbock near the farming community of New Deal, the winery is named for the wild fowl spotted near the vineyard. There are picnic tables and an arbor.

Its vineyards planted in 1979, the family-owned operation is located in an American viticulture area called
Texas High Plains, otherwise known as cotton-growing, Buddy Holly

country. Pheasant Hill and nearby competitors have helped build a solid reputation for Lone Star vintages.

Awards: Silver for '97 Merlot ('00 Lone Star Competition).

South Texas

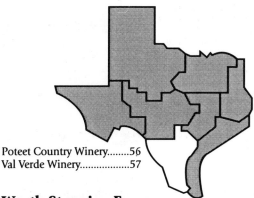

Worth Stopping For:

Poteet Strawberry Festival, *Poteet*, Every April, one of Texas' oldest events provides abundant family entertainment, including concerts, dance troupes, gunslingers, clowns, puppets, regional bands, contests and rodeo performances. (830) 742-8144.

Poteet Country Winery

From San Antonio: Go south 36 miles on Texas 16, right on County Road 478, left on County Road 2145, right on Tank Hollow Road

400 Tank Hollow Road
HC65, Box 19-E
Poteet, Texas 78065
Tel: 830-276-8085
www.poteetwine.com
e-mail: poteetwine@peoplepc.com

Tasting, tours: Friday, Saturday and Sunday, noon - 6 p.m.. Weekdays by appointment.
Varieties: Strawberry, Strawberry Reserve, Mustang Grape, White Mustang, Peach, Blackberry, Pear.

Located 30 minutes south of San Antonio and deep in Texas strawberry country, this establishment produces the "official" wine of the annual Poteet Strawberry Festival.

Founders Jim Collums and Bob Denson say they use only locally grown fruit for their wines. The winery is housed in an old dairy.

The nearby General Store is furnished as a pre-Prohibition mercantile establishment that sells crafts along with the fruit wines and winemaking equipment.

Check the Web site for events, ranging from cook-offs, hayrides and Old West get-togethers to foot-stomping musical events.

Every November, the winery hosts its own Country Wine Festival with live entertainment, Dutch-oven chuckwagon food, "chicken roping," arts and crafts. People come as much for the relaxing country ambience as for the wine. Picnickers are encouraged and the grounds can be hired for special occasions.

Val Verde Winery

100 Qualia Drive
Del Rio, Texas 78840
Tel. (830) 775-9714

Tastings, tours: Mon.-Sat. 9 a.m. to 5p.m.
Varieties: Lenoir, Tawny Port, Merlot,
Sangiovese, Muscat Canelli, Cabernet
Sauvignon, Rose.

Located near the Mexican border, Val Verde is Texas' oldest winery, established in 1883 by Italian immigrant Frank Qualia. Friends were so taken with his wine, made from the Lenoir grape, that he began selling his output.

Fifty years later, the winery began crushing the Herbemont grape grown in its vineyard. Today, the winery is best known for its Don Luis Tawny Port and for the non-union, wild geese that do the weeding. And it's still a family operation.

VAL VERDE WINERY

DON LUIS
Texas
TAWNY PORT

PROPRIETOR'S CHOICE § BLEND NO. 8
PRODUCED AND BOTTLED BY VAL VERDE WINERY
100 Qualia Dr., Del Rio, Tx. 78840 § Alcohol 18% by Volume

Gulf Coast

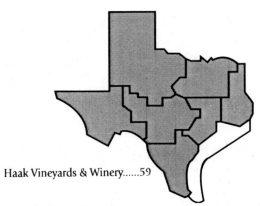

Haak Vineyards & Winery......59

Worth Stopping For:

The Strand, *Galveston*, the island-city's pride is the restored 19th century business quarter lined with boutiques, eateries and gift shops. **Elissa**, a refurbished and seaworthy tall ship, is open to the public at the nearby **Texas Seaport Museum,** which has a souvenir shop whose proceeds benefits the city's historical trust.

Moody Gardens, *Galveston*, Travel the oceans of the world at **The Aquarium at Moody Gardens**. Enjoy the **Rainforest Pyramid** as you walk through thousands of tropical plants, exotic fish and birds. Experience hands-on science at the **Discovery Pyramid**, and explore the universe at the **Ridefilm Theater**. See spectacular images leap from the screen of the six-story **IMAX 3D Theater** and relax on beautiful **Palm Beach**. End your day at **Moody Gardens** with a dinner cruise aboard the **Colonel Paddlewheel Boat.**

Queen Anne B&B, *Galveston*, a Queen Anne-style B&B with gourmet breakfasts and use of bikes to tour the nearby Strand (800) 472–0930.

Stingaree, *Crystal Beach*, for lovers of oysters and beautiful views. (409) 684-2731.

Haak Vineyards & Winery

Located 1.9 Miles west of Texas 6

6310 Avenue T
Santa Fe Texas 77510
Tel. (409) 925-1401
Fax (409) 925-0276
www.haakwine.com

Tastings, tours: In Summer (May-Oct.), Monday-Friday 11:00 a.m.to 6:00 p.m., Saturday 11:00 a.m. to 7:00 p.m., Sunday 12:00 p.m. to 6:00 p.m. In Winter, (Nov.-April) Monday-Friday 11:00 a.m. to 5:00 p.m., Saturday 11:00 a.m. to 6:00 p.m., Sunday 12:00 p.m. to 5:00 p.m. Closed Easter Sunday, Thanksgiving Day, December 25 and January 1
Varieties: Cabernet Sauvignon, Chardonnay, Ruby Port, Bois de Blanc, Sangiovese, Sauvignon Blanc, Syrah, Zinfandel.

Starting as a hobby with two vines in 1975, Raymond and Gladys began what would become the first commercial winery in the unlikely terrain of Galveston County. But the varietal vintages crafted by this electrical engineer and accountant have proved their worth at a slew of state competitions.

They now have an 11,000-square foot winery and 1,800-square foot cellar, with a sump pump keeping seepage from taking over. Now that demand outpaces their 3-acre vineyard's supply, the Haaks bring in grapes from California and Texas growers.

They have catering for special events, a deli and a gift shop. Check their web site for numerous free musical events with catered meals.

Awards: Gold for '00 Cabernet Sauvignon, Bronze for '00 Chardonnay (Wine Societyof Texas/Media Choice Competition); Silver for '01 Texas Chardonnay (2002 People's Choice/ GrapeFest); Silver for 2001 Ruby Port (2003 Texas' Best Wine Competition) Bronze for '01 Blanc du Bois (2002 San Diego National Wine Competition); Silver for '02 Blanc du Bois (2003 GrapeFest People's Choice).

Recipes

Table of Contents

Starters

Paul's Port Pecans
Becker Vineyards, Stonewall

1 cup pecan halves
1 /2 cup sugar
1/4 cup Becker Vintage Port

Combine sugar and port in frying pan on high heat. Stir mixture constantly. As soon as mixture begins boiling, add pecans and continue stirring and turning pecans to prevent burning.

Within five to six minutes, mixture will suddenly become very thick and the port red color will begin to change to a dark caramel color. Remove from heat; drop and separate pecans onto a greased cookie sheet. Use a wooden spoon to push the pecans out of the pan onto the cookie sheet.

NOTE: *Do not touch pecans while cooking or dropping on cookie sheet.*

Pecans should cool in about 15 - 20 minutes.

Eat as a snack like popcorn, crumble on ice cream, add to your favorite salad greens with balsamic vinegar, use as chocolate cake or cheesecake topping or sprinkle on warmed Brie cheese.

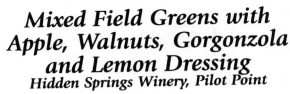

Mixed Field Greens with Apple, Walnuts, Gorgonzola and Lemon Dressing
Hidden Springs Winery, Pilot Point

Salad
2 lbs. mixed field greens
1 /2 cup toasted walnuts
2 Granny Smith apples, peeled abd sliced thinly
1 /2 cup blue cheese or gorgonzola, crumbled
Salt, pepper to taste

Dressing
1 /2 cup extra-virgin olive oil
Juice of 2 lemons
Salt, pepper to taste

Place oil in a chilled bowl and whisk in lemon juice, salt and pepper until blended well. Arrange apple slices on plate; place greens in center of plate; top with walnut pieces and crumbled cheese. Serve with dressing and cracked black pepper

Becker's Onion Soup
Becker Vineyards, Stonewall

1 lb. onions, sliced thinly
1/2 stick butter
2 cans chicken broth, undiluted
1 can beef broth, undiluted
1-1/2 cups water
1 cup white wine, such as Becker

Vineyard's Texas Chardonnay
5 tbsp. flour
1 lb. Swiss cheese, grated
1/4 tsp. pepper
Dry French bread, thickly sliced

Saute onions in butter for 20 minutes or until soft. Add flour, increase heat and stir. Add all liquids and pepper. Simmer for at least 30 minutes. Place French bread slices in soup bowls, top with cheese. Pour hot soup over all.

Entrees

Beef Bourguignon Chez LightCatcher
LightCatcher Winery, Fort Worth

8 oz. bacon, coarsely chopped
3 lbs. boneless beef chuck, out into 1-1/2-inch cubes, trimmed of fat
Salt and pepper
1/3 cup all-purpose flour
Vegetable or olive oil, as needed
1-1/4 lbs. boiling onions, peeled
1 lb. large carrots, peeled, cut into 1-inch slices
12 large garlic cloves, peeled and left whole (do not use 'elephant garlic')
2 12-oz. cans or 3 cups beef broth
1/2 cup brandy (cheap is fine)
2 750 ml bottles red wine (Traditionally used is a red Burgundy, which is really Pinot Noir. A good Pinot can be expensive and is also perhaps a little delicate for this cooking. A hearty Burgundy jug wine will do)
1 lb. mushrooms, halved
1/3 cup chopped fresh thyme, or 2 tbsp. dried
1 tbsp. brown sugar
1 tbsp. tomato paste

Preheat oven to 325F. Saute bacon in a heavy, large Dutch oven over medium-high heat until brown and crisp and fat is rendered. Remove bacon; leave fat.

Rub salt and pepper into beef cubes, then shake in baggie with flour to coat. Use all of the flour. Working in three batches, brown beef in bacon fat over high heat, about 5 minutes per batch. Remove all beef to large bowl. Add onions and carrots to same pot, saute until light brown (add a little more oil if needed.) Add garlic, saute about a minute (do not brown).

Remove all vegetables to bowl with beef. Add 1 cup of broth and all brandy to pot; boil until reduced to glaze, scraping up browned bits, about 8 minutes. Return meat, juices and vegetables to pot. Add wine, mushrooms, thyme, sugar, tomato paste and 2 cups of broth. Bring to boil, cover and place in oven. Cook until beef is tender, about 1-1/2 hours.

Remove pot from oven. Ladle liquid from pot into separate saucepan. Spoon off fat. Boil liquid until reduced to about 2-1/2 cups, about 40 minutes. Pour liquid back over beef and vegetables. Stir.

The dish can be made one day ahead, refrigerated, and rewarmed over low heat before serving. It also freezes well. Serve with freshly baked bread; we prefer an artisan loaf baked with dill and onion . Then we pair it with our LightCatcher Winery Texas Roads Cabernet Sauvignon or Merlot.

Beef Tenderloin Stuffed with Tomato Cilantro Paste
Fall Creek Vineyards, Tow

3-1/2 to 4 lb. beef tenderloin, trimmed of fat and sinew, at room temperature
1/2 cup olive oil
2 tbsp. balsamic vinegar
Salt, pepper
Tomato cilantro stuffing (see below)

Whisk oil and vinegar together and pour over tenderloin. Marinate for 1-2 hours.

Pour off marinade and cut a deep slit in the center down the length of the tenderloin. Salt and pepper tenderloin. Stuff the slit or pocket with the tomato cilantro mixture.

Place stuffed tenderloin uncovered on a rack in roasting pan. Roast at 400F. approximately 35 minutes for medium rare.

Tomato Cilantro Stuffing

1 tbsp. unsalted butter
4 tbsp. chicken broth
3 tsp. garlic, minced

1/4 cup salt
6 tbsp. tomato paste
4 tbsp. cilantro, minced

Saute garlic in butter. Add tomato paste, broth and salt to garlic butter and cook until mixture thickens. Remove from heat and stir in cliantro. Makes 8 servings.

Enjoy with Fall Creek Vineyards Merlot

Spicy-Braised Lamb Roast
Pleasant Hill Winery, Brenham

6 garlic cloves, minced
1 tbsp. plus 1 tsp. thyme leave
1 tbsp. cumin seeds
2 tsp. finely chopped rosemary
1 star anise
2 tsp. fine sea salt
1 tbsp. coriander seeds
1 tsp. coarsely ground white pepper
5-lb. lamb roast, preferably from the hip section
1/4 cup extra-virgin olive oil
3 cups Pleasant Hill Collina Bianca

Preheat the oven to 300F. Combine the garlic, spices and other seasonings.

Cut slits in the meat and rub the mixture all over the lamb, working it into the slits.

In a medium roasting pan, heat the oil. Add the lamb and brown it on all sides over moderate heat. Add the wine and cover pan. Transfer roast to oven and braise the lamb in the oven for 2-1/2 hours, or until very tender. Baste as necessary to prevent it from drying out.

During the last half-hour, remove the lid to reduce juices. Transfer the lamb to a carving board. Strain the cooking juices through a fine sieve; skim the fat. Transfer the juices to a gravy boat. Slice the lamb and serve with the juices. Makes 8 servings.

Basil Shrimp Pasta
Fall Creek Vineyards, Tow

1/3 cup minced green onion
4 garlic cloves, minced
2 tbsp. butter
1 lb. shrimp, peeled
1 tbsp. raspberry vinegar
2 tbsp. minced fresh basil
Salt, pepper

Pasta and Sauce
10 oz. fettucini
1 /2 cup butter
8 oz. cream
3/4 grated fresh Parmesan cheese

Saute onion and garlic in butter. add shrimp and cook until tender. Remove from heat and sprinkle shrimp with vinegar and basil. Toss to mix well. Salt and pepper to taste.

Cook pasta al dente. Prepare sauce by slowly cooking butter, cream and cheese over medium heat until all ingredients are well-integrated with creamy texture. Toss pasta with sauce and serve hot, topping each serving with shrimp mixture.

Serve with Sauvignon Blanc.

Pork Loin with Travis Peak Select Muscato Blanco Vegetable Sauce

Flat Creek Estate Winery, Marble Falls

Flat Creek Estate owner Rick Naber loves to prepare foods on the grill. He also loves experimental dishes and created this sauce for a Fourth Friday at Flat Creek Estate, a celebratory evening for the whole Flat Creek family.

6 1-inch thick butterflied pork loins
1-1/2 cups grated carrots
3/4 cup diced sweet onion
1/4 cup each butter and olive oil
2 cups of Travis Peak Select Muscato Blanco
(pour the remaining amount for the chef)
1/2 tsp. coriander
1/2 tsp. seasoned salt
1/2 tsp. allspice
2 tbsp. brown sugar

2 tbsp. maple syrup

Grill pork loins (seasoned to your taste) on the grill.

Saute onions and carrots in butter and olive oil until onions are clear and carrots soft in texture. Add remaining ingredients and simmer on low heat until the sauce is the consistency desired for serving. (If tempted to add a pinch of this or a dash of that, know that Chef Rick does the same.) Serve over pork loins.

Excellent served with buttered red potatoes and steamed asparagus.

Chicken Rollatine with Proscuitto de Parma, Spinach & Cheeses
Hidden Springs Winery, Pilot Point

4 chicken breast halves
8 very thin slices Prosciutto
1/4 lb. sliced cheese (Muenster, Swiss, mozzarella, Monterrey Jack, grated Parmesan and/or grated Romano)
1 bunch spinach
Salt, pepper to taste
Fresh basil (optional)
Seasoned flour
Olive oil

Pre-heat oven to 400F. Using meat mallet, pound each chicken breast until very thin, being careful not to tear. Season and place 1 slice of ham, spinach, cheese and another slices of ham on chicken.

Roll jelly-roll fashion, then drench in flour and pan fry in enough oil to cover bottom, being careful to sear all sides. Put in an ovenproof casserole dish and finish in a 400F oven for 5 minutes.

Remove and slice in thirds and serve with marinara or your favorite sauce.

Serve with Hidden springs Chardonnay, Sauvignon Blanc or Crystal Red, or similar

Poached Salmon Steaks with Lemon Cream Basil Sauce

Messina Hof, Bryan

6 salmon steaks
4 tbsp. butter or margarine
1 tsp. salt
2 shallots, finely chopped
1 tbsp. lemon juice
2 bay leaves, quartered
1/2 cup Messina Hof Chardonnay
1-1/2 tbsp. flour
2 tbsp. heavy cream
Chopped basil

Preheat oven to 400F. Wash the salmon steaks and dry on paper towels.

Spread 2 tablespoons of butter in a medium baking dish. Place the salmon in dish and sprinkle with salt, shallots, lemon juice and bay leaves. Pour Chardonnay over each steak. Cover baking dish with aluminum foil and bake for 15 minutes.

Baste steaks with drippings from dish; cover and bake for 10 minutes longer or until salmon flakes easily with a fork.

Carefully remove fish from the baking dish and drain well. Strain and reserve one cup of drippings from dish.

Arrange steaks on heatproof serving platter or

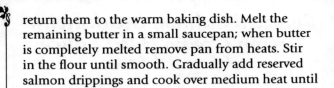

return them to the warm baking dish. Melt the remaining butter in a small saucepan; when butter is completely melted remove pan from heats. Stir in the flour until smooth. Gradually add reserved salmon drippings and cook over medium heat until thickened. Carefully stir in cream.

Pour sauce over salmon steaks. Place your completed dish in the broiler for 3 to 5 minutes or until golden brown. Sprinkle with basil and top with lemon rind curl. Makes 6 servings.

Coq au Vin chez LightCatcher
LightCatcher Winery, Fort Worth

tbsp. olive oil
8 chicken thighs, skin on, trimmed of fat and extra skin
1 large yellow onion, diced
2 carrots, peeled and sliced
5 fresh thyme sprigs, or 1 tablespoon dried
2 small bay leaves
1 tbsp. whole black peppercorns
2 tbsp. chopped garlic
1 750ml red wine1 tbsp. sugar

8 oz. bacon slices, out into 1-inch pieces
1 lb. mushrooms, halved
6 oz. pearl onions (about 1-1/2 cups) or small boiling onions, blanched two minutes in boiling water, peeled
1 tbsp. all purpose flour
Chopped fresh parsley (optional)

Heat oil in heavy deep skillet over medium-high heat. Sprinkle chicken with salt and pepper. Add to skillet in two batches and brown well, turning after 6 minutes, for a total of about 12 minutes each batch. Remove chicken.

Add onion, carrot, bay, thyme and peppercorns and saute briefly until light brown. Add garlic and saute one minute but do not brown. Return chicken to skillet. Add wine and sugar. Bring all to boil. Cover, lower heat and simmer until chicken is cooked through, turning once, about 40 minutes.

Cook bacon in separate skillet until crisp and brown. Remove bacon with tongs, leaving fat in pan. Add mushrooms and pearl onions, reduce heat to medium and saute until onions are tender, about 10 minutes. Tip skillet and pull vegetables to side out of fat.

75

Use tongs to transfer chicken to bowl or pan; tent with foil. Strain the sauce into a bowl (a chinois strainer works best). Let sauce sit until fat moves to top, then remove all fat but put one tablespoon of fat back into skillet.

Put flour into fat and make a roux (cook flour in fat until a paste is formed).

Return sauce to skillet slowly while incorporating into roux. Boil until reduced to about 2 cups, whisking often, about 8 minutes. Mix in mushrooms and onions. Place chicken pieces on a plate, then spoon sauce over. Sprinkle with crumbled bacon and parsley.

Serve with oven-roasted potatoes. Pair with our LightCatcher Winery's Texas Roads Merlot or similar.

Desserts

Toasted Pecan Pie with Orange Sauce
Fall Creek Vineyards, Tow

Crust
1-1/4 cup Wondra flour
1/4 tsp. salt
6 tbsp. cold unsalted butter, cut into bit
2 tbsp. corn oil
3 tbsp. ice water

In large bowl, mix flour and salt and cut in cold butter. Blend in corn oil and ice water and toss mixture to form ball. Knead dough lightly to distribute fat evenly and re-form into ball. Dust dough with flour and roll out to fit tart pan.

Chill dough in tart pan for one hour or more. Line shell with foil and weight with rice or beans. Bake 15 minutes at 400F. Remove crust from oven and reduce heat to 375F. Remove foil and rice and put pie crust back in oven for 5 more minutes to brown bottom of crustsp.   Remove from oven. Bake 25 to 30 minutes until filling is setsp.

Pie Filling
1/2 cup dark brown sugar
2 tbsp. flour
1/2 tsp. salt
2 tbsp. melted butter

8 oz. sour cream
1/2 cup white corn syrup
1/4 cup maple syrup
1 tsp. vanilla
4 eggs
1-1/2 cup toasted pecan pieces
1 cup toasted pecan halves

In large bowl, mix brown sugar, flour and salt. Add butter, sour cream, both syrups, vanilla and eggs. Mix well. Fold in pecan pieces and pour into partially baked pie shell. Place pecan halves in concentric circles on top. Bake 25 to 30 minutes until filling is set.

Orange Sauce
1 cup sugar
2 tbsp. cornstarch
1/4 tsp. salt
2 cup boiling water
2 tbsp. butter
2 tbsp. grated orange rind
6 tbsp. fresh orange juice
2 tbsp. fresh lemon juice
1 tbsp. Grand Marnier

Mix sugar, cornstarch, salt and gradually stir in boiling water. Cook over low heat until thickened and clear, stirring constantly. Remove sauce from heat and stir in butter, rind and juices. Serve with pecan pie. Makes 3 cups.

Serve with Johannisberg Riesling

White Chocolate Pecan Pie
Hidden Springs Winery, Pilot Point

1 9" pie shell, pre-made or homemade
3 eggs
1 cup pecan pieces
3/4 cup white chocolate, broken into small pieces
1 /2 cup ???
Pinch of Salt
1 tbsp. flour
1 cup dark corn syrup

1 /2 tsp. vanilla extract

Preheat oven to 450F. Brush pie shell with 1 beaten egg. Evenly distribute pecans and chocolate on pie shell.

Mix all remaining ingredients well and pour into shell, careful to coat each pecan.

Place in 450F oven for 5 minutes. Turn over to 350F and continue to cook until filling is firm and set, about 40 to 45 minutes.

Serve with Hidden Springs Texas Velvet or Hidden Springs Ruby Glow

Chocolat Cabernet Torte
Comal Creek Winery

Macadamia nut crust:
10 oz. unsalted macadamia nuts or hazelnuts (about 2-1/2 cups)
1/4 cup sugar
4-1/2 tbsp. unsalted butter, melted

Cabernet Ganache filling:
18 oz. bittersweet or semi-sweet chocokate, coasely chopped
3/4 cup heavy cream
3/4 cup Dry Comal Creek Cabernet Sauvignon
1/2 cup sour cream
1/2 cup sugar (if using semi-sweet chocolate, or 1 cup if using bittersweet)
2 oz. white chocolate
Dash cinnamon
1 tsp. vanilla

For crust: Preheat oven to 360F. In a food processor
fitted with metal blade, process nuts and sugar 20
to 30 second or until nuts are finely ground. With
motor running, add the melted butter through the
tube and process for 5 to 10 seconds or until the
mixture is just combined.

Scrape mixture into 11-inch tart pan with a
removable bottom. Press evenly over the bottom
and sides of tart pan. Bake 20 to 25 minutes until
golden brown. Remove from oven and let cool.

For filling: Place dark chocolate in medium bowl; set
aside. In a small heavy saucepan, whisk together the

cream, wine, sour cream and sugar.

Cook over medium-high heat, whisking constantly until sugar is dissolved and mixture begins to bubble around the edges. Pour the hot cream mixture over the chopped chocolate and let stand for 30 seconds to melt the chocolate. Gently whisk until smooth. Scrape the filling into the tart shell and spread evenly with a small spatula.

Melt the white chocolate. Make a small paper cone with a tiny opening at the tip and fill with some of the melted white chocolate. Pipe circles around the inside edge of the filling. Drag a toothpick through the center of each dot to form small heartsp.

Refrigerate the tart for at least 4 hours. Makes 10 servings.

Serve with Comal Creek Cabernet Sauvignon, Cabernet Franc

Camille's Ported Pears
La Buena Vida Vineyards, Springtown and Grapevine

This is great as a first course or as an accompaniment to venison or game bird.

3 large Bartlett or Bosc pears
1/2 cup pear nectar
1/2 cup Walnut Creek Cellars Port
1 tbsp. brown sugar
1 tsp. ground cinnamon
Juice from 1 lemon
1 /2 cup English Stilton or other bleu cheese
1/ 2 cup coarsely chopped walnuts

Heat oven to 350F. Halve the pears, scooping out the cores and stems but leaving the peel. Cut a thin slice from the rounded sides so they sit flat, core side up, and set them in a baking dish.

Mix the pear nectar with half the Port and pour it over the pears. Stir together cinnamon, sugar and lemon juice and sprinkle the mixture over the pears. Bake in the oven for 10 minutes.

Crumble the cheese into a bowl, stir in the walnuts and spoon this mixture into the hollows in the pears, mounding it well. Pour the remaining Port over the cheese and continue baking, basting often, until pears are tender and cheese is brown. Serve over a bed of field greens. Makes 6 servings.

Wine Drinks

Sangria al Flat Creek
Flat Creek Estate, Marble Falls

750 ml of Travis Peak Select Cabernet Sauvignon or equivalent
24 oz. of limemade
2 shots of Brandy
Seasonal fruit, pealed and sliced or cubed

Combine equal parts of Cabernet Sauvignon and limeade. Add two shots brandy and seasonal fruit, using grapes during vintage.

If individual servings are desired: Place ice in glass. Add 2 ounces of club soda. Fill glass with the mix and a splash of lemon. Float desired fruit and serve.

Note: If serving a group, combine all ingredients in a pitcher. Serve immediately.

White Sangria
Cross Roads Vineyards, Cross Roads

750 ml bottle of Cross Roads Vineyards Muscat Canelli or equivalent
1 orange
1 lime
1 lemon
1 small can of crushed pineapple
1 peach
1 liter of 7UP or ginger ale
1 cup sugar

Mix well and serve with lots of ice.

For red sangria, use Cross Roads' Dulce de Rosa

Index of Wineries

>==·!·<>·=·O·=·<>·!·==<

Great Texas books: 'Small size, big taste'
– *Galveston Daily News*

Cordon Bubba Texas Cuisine Real down-home Lone Star recipes. "Just perfect" – *Wichita Falls Times Record News*. 80 p. paperback. ISBN 1-892588-005. $5.95 List

Texas Braggin' Rights Winning recipes of the best Texas cook-offs, includes dishes that took top honors. "Texana for foodies!" -- *D magazine*. 80 p. paperback. ISBN 1-892588-01-3. $5.95 List

Tex Mex 101 "From family favorites to gourmet creations, recipes from Texans who know" – *Sherman-Denison Herald News*. 80 p. paperback. ISBN 1-892588-02-1. $5.95 List

Texas Morning Glory Memorable recipes from bed and breakfast inns. "A delightful little book; rise and dine!" – *Texas Highways*. 88 p. paperback. ISBN 1-892588- 07-2. $5.95 List

Salsa! Salsa! Salsa! Crystal Walls' guide for every-occasion salsas. "Hottest book on the shelf" – Bud Kennedy, *Fort Worth Star-Telegram*. 88 p. paperback. ISBN 1-892588-05-6. $5.95 List

Sources: *Texas Wineries* is based on information from the winemakers as well as publications and on-line reference materials of the Texas Department of Agriculture, the Texas Hill Country Wine & Food Festival, the Texas Wine Marketing Institute of Texas Tech University and the Texas Wine & Grape Growers Association.